THIS SIDE OF THE PAST

OF THE PAST

Alaska's Port Alsworth

D1291829

THIS SIDE
OF THE PAST

Alaska's Port Alsworth

DORIS
HAGEDORN

XULON PRESS ELITE

Xulon Press Elite
2301 Lucien Way #415
Maitland, FL 32751
407.339.4217
www.xulonpress.com

© 2019 by Doris Hagedorn

All rights reserved solely by the author. The author guarantees all contents are original and do not infringe upon the legal rights of any other person or work. No part of this book may be reproduced in any form without the permission of the author. The views expressed in this book are not necessarily those of the publisher.

Unless otherwise indicated, Scripture quotations taken from the New King James Version (NKJV). Copyright © 1982 by Thomas Nelson, Inc. Used by permission. All rights reserved.

Printed in the United States of America.

ISBN-13: 978-1-54565-922-9

Acknowledgements

Our families, friends and supporters merged with the grace, mercy and love of God to make this book possible. We are thankful to our Lord and Savior Jesus Christ and all who prayed for years hoping to see this book completed. In fact, it has merely begun with volumes 1 and 2. Lord willing, there will be more volumes, for the mission girls have been in Alaska nearly sixty years.

Thanks to all who lived their story!

To the Alsworth family and people of Port Alsworth, AK.

To all who provided info, pictures, editing and encouragement.

To artist and pilot-friend, Jeff W. Disney for the unique cover artwork.

To Katherine Meyers, National Park Service, Anchorage, AK. and John Branson/National Park Service, Port Alsworth, AK.

To the Native people of Alaska—who will always have a special place in our hearts!

BIOGRAPHY

Florence Hicks, born and raised in Lansing, MI, graduated from Holt High School and Grand Rapids School of the Bible and Music. Flo was a great fan of baseball, and pitched softball fast-pitch for a women's home-town team. She worked her way through school, and was accepted by Arctic Missions, Inc. (1959) for ministry in Alaska—quick to share her skill "on ice!"

Doris Hagedorn, born and raised near Vancouver WA; home community Fargher Lake, graduated from Battle Ground High School and Multnomah School of the Bible—now Multnomah University—Portland, OR.

She was accepted by Arctic Missions, Inc. (1960) for village work among the native people of Alaska. Doris and her co-worker, Florence Hicks have worked in Alaska for nearly 60 years, serving under Arctic and InterAct Ministries. Retirees in service to our Lord, Doris and Flo's personal stories, at the insistence of friends, will be detailed in Volume III, "Forget-me-not-Blue".

TABLE OF CONTENTS

Babe and Mary Alsworth and family.
(L to R) Lonnie, John, Babe, Mary, Glen, Margaret, Bee

GRANDPA'S STRONG HANDS

What an interesting experience, not only the flight through Lake Clark Pass, but also meeting an incredible family! Dean, our mission pilot, set the plane down just fine, though we bumped quite a bit; the runway wasn't smooth like the city airport! One was almost forced to sit down at Port Alsworth, for all that bumping around even in the air makes you look for a restroom! How fun to meet the Alsworth family! I had no idea the coming years would form such a bond of respect, appreciation and Christian love.

Speaking of respect, I view Mary as a true home-maker. She kept a strong hand of control, yet the kids were free and happy! I think her kitchen and food had a lot to do with that! I don't remember her spanking her own children, but she probably didn't have to! I'm thinking she may have had a paddle *handy*, but these were the days when a word firmly spoken, was effective!

Grandpa? I don't remember him lifting his voice louder than normal! I do remember one incident when John and Glen crawled up on the table to grab a pancake, or when they tried to show me Grandpa's Tell and See machine, tinkering with it—trying to make it work. Grandpa walked into the dining room and caught them red-handed! Says Grandpa in a low, calculated, thoughtful manner: "Now if that machine doesn't work when I get back, you're both going to get a spanking!" The boys climbed off the table, fidgeted a bit and grew quiet. They had on their hickory-striped bib overalls, and they loved company! To make a longer story short, Grandpa bent them over one at a time and gave each two calculated, solid swats to the seat of learning! He didn't have to say a word, either! It was called *correction*. They owned a lot of respect for their father—throughout their lives. I'm reminded of a Bible Chapter and Verse: Proverbs 22:6 "Train up a child in the way he should go, And when he is old he will not depart from it." *When I read chapters 12 and 13, I want to keep on reading. In fact, Proverbs has enough chapters for a whole month— one a day! I truly believe it would do us all good to apply such good advice, don't you? Anyone that finds themselves in trouble can't afford to ignore the book of Proverbs. It holds the answers to life.*

Leon and Sig in Grandpa's arms

A Home For Leon And Sig

*L eon III, you are the son of Leon Jr. (Lonny) and
Martha; the Grandson of Leon Sr. (Babe) and
Mary. Thank you for the privilege of sharing this
small portion of your story.*

Sig was born in 1965, about a year and a half after
his brother, Leon III—*that's you*! Though Leon and
Sig were much alike, we always thought Sig developed a few traits of his maternal grandfather, Dick
Bedell, both in looks and in his whimsical way. We
remember meeting your Grandpa Dick, Grandma
Jean, Aunt Carol and Martha (your Mother.) There
was your younger Uncle Steve, and I remember
mention of your Great-Grandmother, though I don't
remember her name. The Bedell family lived at Port
Alsworth for a while, having purposely moved out
of Anchorage. Dick was invited to teach the Gospel
Message from time to time, which he gladly did—
from Babes living room—and his daughters played
hymns on their violin, which they both played
beautifully. In time, Dick went on down to Bristol

Bay for work. Eventually, the family returned to their original home in California—except for your mother Martha, who married and stayed in Port Alsworth *to bring Leon and Sig into the world!*

Both of your grandfathers were pilots, and it was no surprise to see Grandpa Babe develop a flying family! After all, the airplane proved such a needful means of transportation for Alaska, and especially for the rural bush areas. It was easy to assume *Leon and Sig could grow up to fly.*

Lonnie would occasionally fly his wife, Martha, and their sons to a nearby village, drop them off for a visit—then continue with his round-trip business flight to Iliamna or elsewhere. He would carry Leon III piggy-back-style on his shoulders. Leon III loved that position—little arms tightly wrapped around his Daddy's head or neck. He loved the safe vantage point! I'm sure others enjoyed the scene as much as we—father with shouldered son, happily striding down the village trail. (Infant Sig, still wrapped in blankets, would be with his Mother up the Lake.)

Lonnie and Martha had their own log-cabin home, built beside beautiful, glacial-green Lake Clark, and within walking distance of Babe and Mary's homestead farm. Some people view bush-life a privilege, while others view it as an un-sought level of difficulty. Most people wouldn't argue with modern convenience of running water and electricity (city style.) Others prefer harder work for the privilege of drinking water free of chlorine! Perhaps it is a trade-off. There are many contrasts between village and city life, as weather can be wonderful—or wild. One can appreciate the beautiful scenery and the privacy of life—or resent the isolation. One can enjoy subsistence-living—or miss the supplied amenities of a city grocery store. Some people need wilderness living—while others feel the need of modern-city convenience. Some, no matter where they live, can feel lonely and depressed, closed in with what old timers call *cabin fever*—or enjoy their surroundings and feel privileged and *free!*

Whatever the reason, we may never know, but the day came when two little boys were dropped off at our village—their Mama disappearing into the big city of Anchorage. Babe and Mary were notified by radio, and promptly flew down to the village to pick up Leon and Sig, (their first grandchildren) whose care—whenever Lonny was flying—would largely fall to them. What a surprise and shock to realize Mama wasn't returning. Grandma and Grandpa's house would soon become home to Leon and Sig. Thankfully, the boys accepted a measure of attention and love—not only from family, but from many others who cared and could help them look forward.

Lonny and Martha with Leon and Sig

Pilots And Planes

Your Dad (Lonny) and Uncle Bee had become skilled pilots, developing their own acrobatic maneuvers. Uncle Bee flew his plane with perfection, while Lonny flew with an ever-present element of venture and surprise. One could often tell from afar which of the brothers were in the pilot seat. However, neither Lonny nor Bee—skilled as they were—had one over on your seasoned Grandpa Babe!

We had often heard it said, "Babe could land on a dime if he had to." We had heard that statement from a number of people! Meanwhile, Babe reminded us, "There are old pilots and bold pilots, but there are no old, bold pilots." We thought Babe one of the best bush-pilots we knew, and we admired his flying skill. A good flying reputation among pilots of Alaska is truly earned. Babe, through many years, had been entrusted with precious live cargo, and though he knew his sons handled their planes in a skillful manor, he would occasionally shake his head over some practiced acrobatics that honed that skill.

Planes and pilots draw much attention among Alaska's people. They hold a very important place in history, and in our daily living. They have moved people, food, supplies, equipment and about anything else you can think of. Years back, people would walk the rugged trails, taking months or years of time just to meet needs of their family, tribe or clan. The dog-team was used when possible, and even they have their place in history. Some of our village friends used *pack-dogs* to carry basic supplies up the mountain, or along the trapping trail. One can long for the olden days when living seemed less complicated. Yet, we forget the harsh times when there was starvation, disease and death—with little medical intervention to span the time and distance. Thankfully, people native of our land were able to use the wild plants, berries, fish, moose—and other resources. We treasure the stories they have shared with us. As a child, our neighbor Ruth remembered her mother portioning out a sliver of dry-fish in an effort to quench their hunger pangs and ward off starvation. That little sliver was to be eaten very slowly, and when necessary, the short supply was stretched and rationed until the next season.

Yes, air travel has made big changes, even for our *spiritual* well-being! People of many backgrounds and religious persuasions have taken a plane through Lake Clark Pass. There were long-ago-prophets and priests of Bible times who did a lot of *walking*. Today there are priests, preachers— oh yes, and missionaries, who *travel by air!* The Alsworth family was quite impressed by a travelling Gospel Preacher named Wally Zwemke, born in 1916, and from Wilmar, MN. Wally not only taught the Scriptures, but also used his well-played accordion and slight-of-hand magic tricks to help folk understand, and to impress Biblical truths on the mind of his listeners. He loved to give the Gospel Message (*John 3:16, John 14:6*) and introduce people to Jesus. Wally presented Babe and Mary's family a one-each-booklet called *Four Spiritual Laws*, which portrayed several Bible verses including Romans 6:23 *"For the wages of sin is death, but the gift of God is eternal life in Christ Jesus our Lord."* Babe was impressed, and offered to fly Wally to several Alaskan villages, for Wally had hoped to reach *all* of Alaska's villages— which seems an impossible undertaking if you look at a map! At the time, Harlan and Avanelle Willis were resident missionaries at near-by Nondalton,

Alaska, working under Arctic Missions, Inc. (1961). Pilot Dick Bedell had flown them in a yellow SR-5 which was named *The Yellow Turkey*. Another story when the Willis family made a pit-stop at Tyonek, young son Steve found it hard to adjust his suspenders sufficiently. Mom Avanelle taught him to "*cwossem*". Steve grew up to become a pilot. Steve's wife Jeanie and I took a ground-school course together from University of Alaska—the teacher? Steve! Without Steve and Jeanie, Doris would not have that certificate sporting a B minus!!!

Steve's Dad, Harlan, was not only a missionary, but also a self-employed line-man and pilot and fisherman. Avanelle did a good job caring for the family at home. Once, when the weather was violent, really violent, and baby was due, she was ready to head for Anchorage. She'd be flown to Iliamna, and take Pacific Northern Airlines (PNA), a two-prop plane from there. Weather didn't clear, and flights were cancelled. Avanelle sent word to Faith Gray, a nurse stationed at Pedro Bay, asking if she could come over and help—in case she couldn't get to Anchorage in time. The weather was wild at Pedro Bay, too. Faith didn't know that she could make it. She waited until she finally saw a smaller plane bouncing around the sky, landing on the wild water in front of the small chapel where she lived. Who would risk such a flight?? A former stunt-pilot, of course! One who knew his plane—and the weather—Babe! He was able to set the plane down at Nondalton where Faith could sit with Avanelle to calm her down. Weather cleared by morning, and Avanelle was able to endure and reach the Anchorage hospital in time. The Willis family raised eight children, including a set of twins, serving thirty years in Alaska under Arctic Missions, Inc. They *served the Lord with gladness*; owned bright smiles and had a great sense of humor! *Babe was one of the best pilots we've known, and many agree!*

Wally Zwemke visits Daniel, Denise, and David Clum.

Harlan and Avanelle Willis family

13

Leon II, Wayne, Margaret, John And Glen

Mary was a very hard worker, and as any hard-working Mom, could be cranky and harsh—perhaps feeling she *earned the right*! When we first met Mary, (1960) I personally thought she was the toughest woman I'd ever met. As her son Bee recently said, *"well, that's the way it really was back then! But when Mom turned to Christ, it was a 100% change!"* *(*That reminds me of the Apostle Paul *(Saul's conversion in Acts 9:1-31.)*

Just to be clear, it is *God's power* that saves, and *God's Word by God's Spirit* that enlightens. Our Lord Jesus used *parables* to help us understand *His* teachings. Example: Luke Chapter 15 gives us *The Parable of the Lost Sheep, the Lost Coin, and the Parable of the Lost Son*. Luke Chapter 16 gives us *The Parable of the Unjust Steward*. Why did Jesus used them as teaching tools? *"Faith cometh by hearing, and hearing by the Word of God"* Romans 10:17. *"All Scripture is given by inspiration of God"* II Timothy 3:16.

Grandpa Babe, greatly impressed by Rev. Wally's clear teachings of the Scriptures, decided Mary needed to hear the well-illustrated Message, and flew her to the near-by village where Wally was holding a week of meetings. Babe dropped Grandma Mary off to visit and attend the meetings—saying he would pick her up after she *got saved.* On February 15, 1961, Mary responded to God's invitation and invited Jesus Christ into her life as Lord. She asked Him to take away all her bad habits. She was instantly released from her addiction to smoking, her language changed, and it was easy to see the difference Jesus made in her life. On February 19, 1961 Babe lined the kids up at their home table, and they too, with his approval, made individual decisions to accept Christ.

June 4, 1961 Babe, Mary and their five children were publicly baptized in Six Mile Lake—an outward confession of their inward faith. Though the waters were plenty chilly for Rev. Harlan, the hearts of those baptized must have been glad and warm with the reassuring *"peace of God which passes all understanding" Philippians 4:7.* After all, their names were written in the *"Lambs book of Life" Revelation 21:27.* What a precious gift—and good for all Eternity! *"If you confess with your mouth the Lord Jesus and believe in your heart that God has raised Him from the dead, you will be saved. For with the heart man believes unto righteousness, and with the mouth confession is made unto salvation" Romans 10:9-13. Jesus said, "I am the resurrection and the life. He who believes in Me though he may die, he shall live. And whoever lives and believes in Me shall never die. Do you believe this?" John 11:25,26.*

Certainly, Mary's comfort was found in reading her Bible and accepting with assurance that her family was safe in Jesus Christ her Lord. The Bible became Mary's daily reading and spiritual food, and was conveniently set next to her kitchen chair—along with her knitting needles and yarn.

SCRIPTURE: *"I am not ashamed of the gospel of Christ, for it is the power of God to salvation for everyone who believes" Romans 1:16. "…without faith it is impossible to please Him, for he who comes to God must believe that He is, and that He is a rewarder of those who diligently seek Him" Hebrews 11:6. "… the Son of Man has come to seek and to save that which was lost" Luke 19:10.*

*"...believe on the Lord Jesus Christ,
and you will be saved, you and your
house (household)" Acts 16:31.*

Speaking of Mary's knitting needles, she was great with Mary Maxum sweaters, knitting one for each of her family, and for Faith, *Flo's first co-worker*, Flo and Doris as well. She then gave us left-over yarn scraps, from which we each knitted a small sweater for niece and nephew—with Mary's help!

Future farmers of Port Alsworth?

Bee, John, Babe, Sis, Glen, and Mary

Freedom To Forgive

Yes, Mary was noticeably changed, making impact on all who met her or sat at her table—but she wasn't weak! When a certain pilot turned his revved-up plane around, a heavy cloud of runway debris and dust covered Mary's newly washed and hung laundry, and she had to do all that huge wash over again! The pilot *heard* from Mary—and I doubt he ever forgot nor let *that* happen again! Of course, Mary was learning to forgive—but it might be a little harder to *forget (grin)!* A radio/tv pastor recently said, "Jesus didn't come to *shame* sinners, but to *save* sinners." And the Lord is still working on *all* of us!

> *"Let no corrupt word proceed out of your mouth, but what is good for necessary edification, that it may impart grace to the hearers. And do not grieve the Holy Spirit of God, by whom you were sealed for the day of redemption. Let all bitterness, wrath,*

*anger, clamor and evil speaking be
put away from you, with all malice.
And be kind to one another, ten-
derhearted, forgiving one another,
even as God in Christ forgave you"
Ephesians 4:29-32.*

Babe said of his son John, "Of all the boys, John
has the best feel for flying." The responsibility for
John's early training had been turned over to his older
brother, Wayne (Bee), and Glen's to John. At 12 or 13
years, the legs needed to be long enough to reach the
foot controls. All but Glen soloed in winter-time, on
skis. Glen had to wait, and soloed on floats. According
to John, John's own solo-*float*- flight took Doris to
Iliamna—landing on Slop Bucket Lake!

One day, a young lady named Esther was con-
versing with Babe. A plane flew in from Bristol Bay.
Babe exclaimed, "That must be Glen, because John
doesn't bounce on landing that way!" Though Esther
didn't realize it then—that scene was her introduction
to John—her future husband. John, his wife Esther
at his side, operates *Alaskan Aircraft Engines, Inc.*
in Anchorage, AK. John—with his enjoyment and
choice of *mechanics* over flying—has maintained
a quality business of his own since 1977. Both Bee

and John maintain their skill. Pilots flying Alaska's skies have depended on their work for years.

Now what about Margaret, called Sis!? She tells me the following stories:

"Dad said, "Whoever learns to milk goats first will learn to *fly* first." I learned to milk goats, but I wasn't taught to fly. I did learn to skin a moose! Dad shot a moose up the creek, brought it home, hung it in the hangar and told Bee and I to skin it. He got in the t-craft and flew away. He came home when we were down to the neck. He finished it!"

"Dad was good at making good fudge, in an iron skillet on the wood-stove!"

Dad's Fudge:
2 Cups Sugar
1/8 tsp Salt
2 Squares Unsweetened Chocolate (equals 2 oz)
(new-box-packaging of 4-pieces equals ½ oz)
1 Cup Evaporated Milk

Place above ingredients in iron skillet, on hot wood-stove, using draft for heat-control. Bring to boil, until moderately heavy bubbles, but don't burn. You may test by dropping a drop of fudge in cold water, and see if it reaches a moderate to hard-ball stage. Also, too much stirring while cooking will make the fudge grainy. When done, add 1 TBS Vanilla. Beat and keep beating. Cool some, and add 1 cube or ½ cube Butter, and continue to beat. When it begins to thicken more, add some Walnuts—unless you are allergic to nuts! Pour fudge into a buttered dish or pie pan before it hardens to an un-pourable stage. When set, cut into squares, and serve. If this recipe turns out for you, enjoy! Limit yourself if you can! (We cannot be responsible for any failure on your part to do so.) We cannot be responsible for any medical issues nor allergies you or your guests may have! We know it is easy to over-indulge on this wonderful fudge! Thank you, Grandpa Babe!

"At times my Dad would add raisins—he knew his kids didn't like them and wouldn't eat them." (Well!! Would you rather have *moose nuggets*?!)

Munching Moose

STORIES BY SIS

"Every October, we would help Dad with our winter wood supply. He would say some things like: *Kids go deep into the forest.* Dad and Lonny would work wood in the mornings, and Bee and I in the afternoon. We would go deep into the forest—out by Tanalian River. (Holey Mountain could be seen from the runway, and Martha Mountain on the right—where there was a pass and short-cut to Pedro Bay.)"

"We kids would also go with Dad and Mom to gather winter's supply of cranberries. We'd go on a windy day—not so many gnats and white-sox, for they were very fierce and miserable! (Mosquitoes were bad enough!!) Bee had a small, green, aluminum pail, and I a red one. They were easy to fill. We also flew up the lake in the JR-SR to pick strawberries by invitation, from Brown Carlson's garden! We dumped the berry buckets into a cardboard box marked Darigold Butter. (It had, at one time, held 48 1-pound cans of butter.) When we came down with whooping cough, we had bad nose-bleeds, and we each carried a butter can to use as a spit-trash-can!"

"Dad was away flying a *lot,* but Uncle Mike (Van Degrift) was always around working on the planes or whatever needed his expertise. He would come into the house for his coffee break, and I, as a young child, could sit on his lap as he ate a cookie and sipped his cup of coffee. Uncle Mike was considered a part of our family. I remembered getting a Sears bicycle for my sixth birthday. It was green and white. I wish I still had it! Uncle Mike ordered skates one year, and sleds—for all of us, and though our Dad was gone and working a lot, I remember him bringing me a clip board from Anchorage—which I still have. On one trip from Anchorage, he brought me a parakeet in a cage. Who gave him *that* idea? I wonder to this day why I'd ask for a parakeet!"

"Sam and Aggie Alexie lived across the Lake, and word was received the baby George wasn't breathing! Dad immediately flew over to pick up the baby—and Dick Bedell went along to hold the baby and keep him breathing. (He was wrapped in seven tight layers of blankets which had to be loosened.) They transported him safely to Anchorage, and his life was spared." (We are so blessed to say he lived, and we have enjoyed the family through the years! *Hi George and Liz!!) And now back to Sis:*

Sis didn't need to fly an airplane, for a special pilot and airplane mechanic, Voight Clum, came along and swept Sis (Margaret) right off her feet! Voight had come to Alaska from a Michigan farm. He was in the military stationed at Wildwood (Kenai) in 1956-57, then attended training in Illinois, acquiring a pilot and mechanic license. He returned to Alaska for work, as Alaska had the planes!! He worked for Northern Consolidated Air, and a number of other Airline companies. Voight was flown to Port Alsworth and Iliamna with pilot Chuck C. This is when he met Sis and the Alsworth's. Sis was taking two years of Home-High-School, staying at Len and Marge McMillen's in Iliamna. (Marge being Voight's sister.) Voight and Sis were married in October of that same year. Voight, in time, would own his own business-shop near Lake Hood (Anchorage), where he developed a very credible business. He had chosen a wonderful, capable, well-trained farm-girl in Margaret. They worked hard, loved the Lord and raised twin boys, David and Daniel, who grew up to fly commercial—as did Bee and Betty's son, Wayne Jr. Margaret supplemented Voight's business with a private in-home Day-Care—*for thirty-two years*! Good job, Sis! Good cook, too! (She uses her Mom's yellow birthday cake recipe for her sibling's birthdays each year—along with the 7-minute icing!) Using a number of her Mother's recipe's, she made great meals, and good homemade bread! Guess what? I'm sure Margaret's daughter, Denise, learned to make that good bread too! Denise completed college, became a school teacher, and she and her husband together raised their family. (*After Voight's Home-going to God's House, Margaret took on the humungous task of building a new house, which today is complete and paid for! In today's vernacular, "You Go Girl!!"*)

Aunt Betty was also a great cook, and on our occasional visit, we loved her moose-meat spaghetti and white cake with 7-minute frosting. She always served it when we were hungry, too! She was also able to make Mary's yellow three-layered cake—with the *yellow* frosting! Betty was blessed with her daughter Missy, learning about airplanes and navigation! *You will learn of Babe and Mary's move—to Hawaii! Dick Proenneke had given them a vacation-ticket to HI. Babe liked Hawaii so much—lots of sunshine and fresh fruit, not having to fight the cold, or soak his feet in warm water; not having to bundle up—and perhaps it was easier on the bones! So, they moved, and were there for nineteen years, keeping up with family news via the U.S. Mail, telephone and an occasional visit. We all missed them!*

On one visit back, Grandpa Babe borrowed Bee's plane and gave flying lessons to fifteen or more young people—including Wayne Jr. and his sister Missy (Mary Lorene), and twins, Daniel and David.

To Parents and Grandparents everywhere: *"Behold, children are a heritage from the Lord—a reward—Like arrows in the hand of a warrior, So are the children of one's youth. Happy is the man who has his quiver full of them..." Psalm 127:3-5.*

Aunt Betty—Anchorage

Mary, Flo, Doris, John and Babe—
Grandma and Grandpa off to HI.

Last trip visit to cabin across the Lake—
Finding burial site of first child.

Happy Birthday to you, Sis...
Have you turned 40 yet??
How many years have come and gone
"Since way back when" we met???

We remember back as a little girl
You "packed the pails", "milked goats!!
You were a bundle of energy
Farm-girl! Working hard, like the "Folks"!

You tended chickens and learned to knit
The things a girl should do.
And then one day you met Voight Clum
The man made "just for you"!!

You were his style...with country smile
Home-spun and "best to be had".
God knew it was you who could cook him that stew
And make his heart happy and glad.

Young and bright, a happy sight
You were always true,"true blue"
Keeping the house "just right" for your spouse,
And cooking his "sourdough's", too!!

As house-keeper-cook you always excelled
And as wife, a number one.
But let's not forget the credit you set
As Mother of daughter and sons!

You raise the clan, care for your man,
And open the door on the chores
The children, the friends, the family,
And how many, many, many, many more??

We meet this day to honor you
And let you know we care.
We love you in a special way
And with you want to share.

You've done so much for all of us
Your heart is warm and kind.
But as a FRIEND, you top the list
And to this fact we'll sign.

HAPPY BIRTHDAY TO YOU, SIS
How can we make this rhyme?
We think you must be thirty-five,   ☺
But we'll say it "thirty-nine"!!!

Love,
Doris and Flo

Jesus loves me this I know, for the Bible tells me so.

LEARNING AND SERVING

M ary home-schooled the children through eighth grade, with exception: Lonny stayed with John and Eileen Meggitt at Levelock for first grade; Randy Briggs (Pt. A.) home-schooled Lonny, Wayne (Bee) and Margaret the following school year. Then Mary took over teaching, deciding on the Calvert School Course from Baltimore, MD, because they assigned a personal teacher to the student. (The State could provide a home school course, but without a permanent, personal teacher.) When John and Glen completed the four years with Mary, they spent a couple more years with lodge-owner and school-teacher, Paul and Irene Carlson, at Iliamna—for additional home-schooling. Glen then went on to graduate from *Victory High School,* (then located at mile 95 Glenn Highway, Palmer.) John spent one year in *God's Invasion Army* and married Esther Abrahamson on December 22, 1973. They are presently blessed with two grown sons,

Joel and Tony, both married with families. *Whew! Education paid off!*

Glen, after High School, spent one year at Grand Rapids School of the Bible and Music—where he also acquired his commercial pilots license. He returned to marry Patrice Elliot on July 14, 1974. We've recently learned Leon's Uncle Glen has logged 35,000-plus hours of flight time, and many more non-logged, non-commercial and humanitarian flights—many with Samaritan's Purse, and to at least, twenty-three countries. He is presently Mayor of Lake and Peninsula Borough. Port Alsworth now has a population of two-hundred-plus. Glen and Patty have one son (Glen Jr) four daughters (Menda, Sonnet, Chandelle, and Charis) and over twenty grandchildren—a number of which are adopted and *anchored* at Port Alsworth. Patty and her parents Laddy and Glenda Elliott, and a number of others deserve much credit for their immeasurable help to community—having resided there for years, working and supporting village or farm—giving positive input and care. We remember a number of pilot-and-teacher families as well, who have greatly cared for community. *I tried to name some, and finally decided to leave the list in the Lord's Hand, for He has the true picture and won't leave anyone out!* Then there are the people who served from the villages. There, again, *I couldn't name them without leaving someone out!!* The count would fill pages! (*Tanalian Bible Camp* has a wonderful outreach to young people even *now*, and can be found *on line*.)

Port Alsworth's people have been active for years, providing Retreat Centers, Training Programs, and positive opportunity. Franklin Graham's Samaritan's Purse Organization, along with many interested people from community and otherwise, have provided upkeep and prayer. We are so blessed for the outreach to a number of villages and urban areas as well. Our thanks to the Lord and the many pilots who have been involved flying campers and staff for Tanalian Bible Camp—oh yes, let's not forget spring's yearly Family Conference. We so appreciate *Lake Clark Air*, *Lake and Pen Air*, *Iliamna Air Taxi*, *Den'ina Air*, *Samaritan's Purse*, and many un-named, all of whom have given so many hours and years in flying service. Pilot Mark Lang and his wife Sandy have been at Port Alsworth since 1976, and now manage *Samaritan Lodge Alaska for Operation Heal our Patriots—a wonderful place for intervention, providing counsel and care for couples and families of wounded veterans.*

If we think back a few more years, we'll remember the days when *Don Stump and Danny O'Hara began Teen Camp at Iliamna, then ten years later, with help of others, moved camp to Tanalian! That era of Teen Camp and Fellowship Conference is most memorable to us—people (including us) were recruited and trained for Counselling; Doris ran the Craft Program and Flo the Camp Store. Tanalian Bible Camp and Family Conference has been active ever since! Names are written in the Lamb's Book of Life, and Don, Danny and workers of today would still agree—the glory belongs to The Lord Himself!*

Our thanks to everyone focused and invested in others around the world. Babe and Mary, as we, would be so *blessed* to know of your big heart! Hats off to the 70 plus pilots we have personally known—twenty of whom have flown Flo and Doris! There is so much more—years-worth—that could be said!

Seeing Sis off to Ohio for 9th Grade

Babe And Mary —
The Earlier Years

Leon Alsworth (Sr) was born in Sherburn, Minnesota on April 13, 1909. His parents, Reid and Margaret (Packard) Alsworth, had a large dairy farm. Leon (known as Babe) was one of six boys born into the family. Sadly, Keith died before reaching adulthood. That left Max, Ken, Bill, Lloyd and Leon (Babe) to help their father raise oats, flax, wheat, barley and soybeans. They also had 150 cattle, half dairy cows and half beef cattle. Max and Ken continued to farm. Babe had the opportunity of flying lessons from John Walatka, who taught Babe to fly. Then (unknown to his Mother) he hired on as a *stunt pilot*. I'm told he was also a *wing-walker*! He would dress up as an old lady, climb aboard John Walatka's N13822 Stinson, and away they go! Babe would walk the wing, and after the landing he would climb down and disappear into the crowd—and ditch the old-lady-clothes! Leon was nick-named Babe—for being the youngest—but he was so taken with flying that he went against his folks wishes and hid his small plane amongst the stored and stacked hay bundles on the field. Four-year-old Fred Walatka noticed the wheels of the plane were unpainted and black—not yellow like the rest of the plane, so he proceeded to paint them yellow! Babe gave him a couple paddles and sent him home! Good influence, for they became friends for life! Of course, Fred enjoyed reminding Babe for years to come—and Babe could no longer hide the story of painted rubber tires. Besides, *the cat was already out of the bag*!

Mary Agnes Griechen was born at three pounds, on August 9, 1924, with the help of her Grandmother Marie. There were no doctors there at Pilot Point. Mary's Mother, Aglaphane Tootsie Oda, was Aleut and Russian decent. Mary at birth had a ten-year old sister, Anna, a sister Alice and a young brother Aleck. Later on, Sophie, Eli and Gust Jr. joined the family. Sister Anna attended grade school at the Jesse Lee Home in Unalaska. The Home was moved to Seward, where the State of Alaska sponsored a contest, seeking a design for the state flag. A fellow-classmate of Anna's, Benny Benson, age 13 and native of Alaska, won the contest—designing our Alaska Flag as it is today: eight stars of gold on a field of blue.

Mary's father, Gust (9-30-1883) was from Germany. He didn't like the military rule, so at seventeen years of age, he hopped a steamer and managed to stay hidden until the ship was two weeks out to sea. When he was discovered it was too late for the ship to turn around and take him back. The ship proceeded on to San Francisco. Gust continued from San Francisco, finding his way to Alaska where he met and married. His wife died in childbirth, and in time he married Aglaphane, called Tootsie. He then took his daughter Anna to live with him and Tootsie. Since Anna had been in the Jesse Lee Home (in Unalaska and later the Home was moved to Seward), Tootsie had died with TB of the lung in 1949. Years later, Anna and Benny Benson met again, and Benny became her second husband! *(We remember meeting Benny in Seward at the Jesse Lee Home, and Flo and I met Anna years later at Port Alsworth. Alaska's population has enjoyed singing The Alaska Flag song—many times over.)*

Benny Benson with Annie and Mary.

Grandpa Gust, John, Sis, Bee, and Lonny]

Gust had become a commercial fisherman, earning three cents a fish! He worked as a cannery watchman and had charge of the company store and operation of the cannery. The village of Pilot Point was on the flat tundra, but the mountains were always visible in the distance. In the winter, Gus trapped.

In 1933 the Aniachak Volcano erupted—or was it the Chiginagak Volcano—covering everything with ash. The children at school saw the cloud of ash coming, but the teacher wouldn't allow them to go home early. By 4 p.m. it was too dark and thick for the students to leave. Mary's father, Gust, took coils of rope, anchored them to the cannery, and walked to the school. The students were then able to follow the rope home. (I've heard two interesting tidbits of information: *the Chiginagak Volcano is located at the headwaters of Mother Goose Lake. Aniachak has a lake in the crater where Sockeye Salmon migrate from the Pacific Ocean to spawn.*)

It was necessary to shovel the ash from the roofs to keep them from collapsing. The water, too, was covered with ash, so they sunk barrels near the lake so the water would soak into the barrels. This made it possible to dip water from a supply of covered barrels. It was five years before things started to grow again. (Mary would return years later to find the old house had burned down, and with it some of the grass baskets that she had made as a child.)

Mary attended the village school, and when eight, she started helping her ten-year old brother, Alex, cook breakfast at the cannery. About fifty fishermen ate breakfast there every day during fishing season. The menu was oatmeal, pancakes, eggs, bacon and coffee. Mary was only about three feet tall, so she had to stand on a box to drop the coffee beans into the hopper and grind them by hand.

In 1932 the old school house was condemned on account of the high tides. In the fall the tied constantly endangered the safety of the children and teachers as well as the school property. An appropriation for a new school building was voted by congress in the spring of 1932. Later that year, the old building burned down—but there was no money available to re-build. Living conditions for the teachers was pretty much dependent on individual citizens or private commercial concerns. The school met temporarily in a building erected by the cannery. Mr. and Mrs. Hanson, the school teachers, continued teaching—Mrs. Hanson without pay. (There were only enough funds for one person, but Mrs. Hanson taught the lower grades cooking and sewing, and she nursed the villagers.) They were very involved in village life. They helped organize a village council and a reindeer company. Weekly church services were held without missing a single week, and public programs were given by the school children. An eight-piece orchestra was organized. Medical assistance was rendered 208 times in one year.

By the time Mary was thirteen, she babysat, clerked in the store, did payroll and as needed went out on the scow and tallied fish as they were brought in by boat. She also worked in the post office, fished and did cannery work, or anything else that needed doing. Each summer, she helped her mother cook for fifty to seventy-five men at the cannery. (Fall-time they concentrated on geese and ducks—canning, smoking and salting them for future use. Reindeer meat was purchased from the reindeer herders; there were no moose or caribou in that area at that time.) Mrs. Hanson's instructions must have paid off, for when Mary's Dad, Gust, was launching a ship, his hand was caught and severely cut on a pipe. The cannery had employed a pre-med student to man the emergency first-aid station, but when he saw the blood pouring from Gust's hand—he fainted. Mary took over, applied pressure, dressed the wound, and was credited with saving her father's life.

The first salmon usually appeared in May, and the salmon continued to come until October. There were three huge drying racks on which they could dry enough fish to feed 25 dogs through the winter months. They also dried, smoked, salted, pickled and canned salmon for their own winter food supply.

Mary enjoyed school, working hard to catch up with her older brother—and often out-spelling the whole school in the weekly spelling bee. There were between 30 and 40 children in the elementary school at Pilot Point. After finishing, they were sent to Eklutna (between Palmer and Anchorage) for vocational school. Mary attended at Eklutna for two years, planning to become a nurse. However, her mother fell while hanging smoke-fish, hit a gas can breaking her hip; also causing some unknown internal injuries. Since she refused to go to the government hospital, she died at home. Mary then decided to stay home to care for her father and three younger brothers and sisters. How hard it is to understand tragedy. The kids worked hard, but they also played hard—outdoor sports such as baseball in summer; skiing, skating and sledding in winter. They enjoyed puzzles and indoor games during the long winter nights.

Until 1933, travel was by dog-team or boat. Supplies came from Seattle by boat; mail came by boat—twice a year. Then in 1933, a pilot named Frank Dorbrant arrived at Pilot Point in his "Travel Air" on floats. He gave any of the brave-enough-villagers a ride in the plane. Children would rush down to greet him and help him gas up the plane. At this time the mail started to come via air. Mary often found herself busy in the post office, helping Gust, her postmaster dad. Then there were pilots—awaiting passengers or weather—needing food and lodging, and the Griechen's *hospitable* home often filled with extra people.

Aglaphane (Tootsie) Oda Griechen

Mary with Aunt Anna, Mary with Uncle Aleck,
Mary with Aunt Alice, and Mary with the J5 Piper and pelts

The Jr -Sr Stinson

B abe came north to check out Alaska, and when he returned to Minnesota, he purchased the JR-SR Stinson N13491. In 1938 Babe and brother Lloyd flew N13491 to Alaska.

Babe did a lot of charter flying, especially in the Bristol Bay area. He flew for Del Monte and others, making frequent trips to Pilot Point, flying fishermen in and out. Pilot Point had a custom to meet every plane that landed. Gas, food, housing was provided as needed. Babe and Mary first met in 1940 when a young man climbed the 40 foot-plus flag pole and fell to frozen ground. It was spring breakup; Babe flew in on skis, landing on very dangerous honey-combed ice. The ice stayed intact, but opened up that very afternoon. He had managed to fly the young fellow to Kanakanak hospital where he lingered several days with internal injuries. The doctors were unable to save him. Sad.

Mary was sixteen when Babe flew the Alaska Packers Company Officials in at end of fishing season. Babe and Mary used the opportunity to get better acquainted. (Tootsie had liked him right away. He didn't smoke nor drink, and that made quite an impression on the family.) Babe asked Gust if he could marry Mary. The reply was "Do you think you can get along?" They were engaged before Christmas, and married on January 4, 1941 — in Dillingham, by the Magistrate. John and Lillian Walatka witnessed the marriage.

In the winter of '41 the Laplanders around Johnson Hill were having trouble with wolves killing off the herd. Babe and Mary, flying a J5 Piper, went to help. The wolves would work their way to the center of the herd. As the reindeer milled in a circle, Babe would dive at the herd. The reindeer would scatter, and Mary would shoot at the wolves—from the plane! The most wolves they could take in a day would be four or five. They used a twelve-gage shotgun with double-ought buckshot. They received a bounty for each wolf, plus they could sell the fur. The sixty or so wolves helped pay for their first plane. Babe had a coat of wolf fur made for both he and Mary, and years later, a coat for Bee made of Coyote. Years later, Mary and Sis would each have a blanket made of sheep. *Anyone who would refute the use of fur may like to test their endurance in*

some severe north wind, for chill factor can easily
drop to 50 to 100 degrees below zero!

Babe and Mary lived in Koggiung until May 1,
1942, then moved to a cabin on the north shore of
Lake Clark. On July 12, 1943, their first son, Leon,
was born. He died April 1, 1944. He had contracted
T.B. of the liver—native children being particularly
susceptible at that time. Babe was in Minnesota for
business when the baby became sick. He lived only a
couple of weeks after Babe's return. How sad the loss
of a child! We have no words to deal with this loss,
but a verse comes to mind: *"Surely He has borne our*
griefs and carried our sorrows" Isaiah 53:4.

Search and Rescue

J5 Piper. Teamwork!]

Mary, Babe, and Browny

According to Bee, Babe had owned four of the SR-JRs through the years:

The Stinson N13491 flipped in Northwestern Lake near Naknek airport. Babe sent Mike VanDegrift down to retrieve the plane. The plane had such water damage, that it was never flown again. The floats were transferred to N13459, and the N13491 was dismantled and retired to the woods where the kids used their imaginative flying skills. It is probably there to this day!

The N13459 was most used of the planes. Before purchase by Babe, it had been flown by the Civil Air Patrol—in the lower 48. Babe continued to fly the plane until 1952—It was his main summer job until their move to Hawaii—when he sold it to Fred Walatka. Fred used it several more years. Then Glen bought it to get it back in the family. It is still in Glen's care at Port Alsworth. *Yeah Glen*!

The N13822, was rebuilt and sold by Bee to Fred Walatka. Fred donated it to the Anchorage Air Museum at Lake Hood.

The N13801 was flown up to Port Alsworth from MN in Sept.1952, by Eddie King and Bob Roth. It resides in FL where it was sold to a collector—in pieces.

Oren Hudson, another well-known Alaskan pilot had also owned a dark-blue SR-JR 87-87 Stinson — named the *Black Widow,* N13831 which was the last one off the assembly line. We flew with Oren a few times — in a wigeon, but we don't remember the SR-JR. It seems, Oren took us from Pedro Bay to Nondalton on our first trip there, telling us "You girls won't have it easy here." However, we've known it has been our *privilege* to have those near-thirty-years among the Lake Country people. Oren Hudson was the first resident bush pilot to live in Nondalton. His wife, Ruth, was a registered nurse with Public Health Service – throughout Alaska.

Arctic Missions, Inc. owned and used a blue SR-JR as well, though Flo and I don't remember seeing it. Pilot Alan Franz flew the plane to a number of villages, such as Galena, Nenana, Shagaluk and Tanana. I was also told the story of Dean Thimsen and Maver Roth with building sup-plies for Nondalton and *everything including the kitchen sink,* taking off from Lake Hood /Lake Spenard. They used the whole run, but were unable to lift above the trees. They crashed through the trees at end of the lake, wiping out the plane! The engine was simply too small for the load, as it can be for this plane with big-load capacity.

Naknek Airways: Babe's first business.

JR-SR Stinson N13822

In 1942, Babe and Mary purchased a small cabin from its builder—a pilot, Jim Kennedy. He had lived in the cabin only 18 months, long enough to realize he needed to sell out. The cabin was located on the *north* shore of Lake Clark where the prevailing east wind blew so terribly strong, tunneling *through* Lake Clark Pass. It *slammed* onto that north shore so strongly, it would render aircraft operation virtually impossible! There was a small lake about three miles away from the cabin—where Babe could hike, keeping his planes anchored down and avoid destruction. Nevertheless, when that east wind started to blow, Babe would have to hike the three miles or so, to get to the plane and take off. He would not plan to return until the wind changed directions. So, Babe and Mike started looking for another place. In the summer of 1943, they found the ideal—Hardenbourg Bay on the *easterly* shore of Lake Clark.

In early spring 1944, Babe and skilled pilot-mechanic Mike VanDegrift went out to Minnesota and brought up another SR-JR Stinson—built in Wayne, MI the year of 1933. *There were 87 SR-JR Stinsons crafted at that time*. Babe continued to use that SR-JR Stinson N13459 to transport hundreds of summer cannery workers to and from the numerous villages of the Bristol Bay arena—and often through the pass to Anchorage—on floats. On such flights, he had noticed and wondered—trying to figure out why people built here and there, everywhere *except* the area with space to build, a *sheltered cove* and room to clear and build a 4,000-foot runway. He decided then and there—*he* would be the one to make that happen! *(Babe related this story—and a number of others—to his son, Bee, the day before the stroke that rendered him speechless. Our thanks to Bee for taking his Dad for that drive, and to Babe for the many years of stories that he cared to leave with his son and family—and ultimately to those of us who realize what a treasure and wealth we hold with the stories of life—and especially the stories of Babe and Mary Alsworth! Thank you, Lord!)*

Mike surveyed the place, looked it over; they then started to clear the land. Babe and Mary hired Joe Thompson and he and Mike cleared enough land to build a shop near the water edge, plus enough land for a small house and a short 1500-foot runway. While Babe was busy flying, and others clearing land, Mary was busy with axe and swede-saw cutting wood—clearing a path for the 1500-foot runway, and hauling the wood in for their winter supply. According to Bee, she cleared most of it by herself. Her brother, Al, came to spend the winter, learn to fly and help Mary with the winter wood supply. Whenever Babe landed, Mary would meet the plane with the dog-sled and help haul the supplies back to the house. (*The house? The same building used for Teen Camp Crafts years later. It still stands today!*)

Lumber was bought from Charlie Denison who owned a sawmill and business. By then it was the fall of 1944.

Babe purchased his own sawmill, and flew it in from Alegnigik river, piece by piece. Mike VanDegrift welded it back together. A small scow was built to bring the grader and cat up from the landing (located below Nondalton.) A Ford-Fergerson tractor (from Naknek) was brought up the Kvichak and across Lake Iliamna by boat, hauled over the landing to six-mile lake, then barged on to Lake Clark and the future Port Alsworth. This began the big task of building that 4,000-foot runway! Several cabins changed hands. (Babe and Mary would live on Lake Clark from 1942-1977.) As the years went by, the Post Office was started, and the name Port Alsworth was assigned—and officially established in 1951. Homes were built and families moved in. Jay Hammond had a home at Miller Creek, and during Jay's two terms as

Governor of Alaska, John Branson (NPS) lived there and kept the place for them. (*Lumber for Babe and Mary's big house and hangar, was purchased from Denison's, who owned a sawmill and business. After purchase it was sawed and planed with tongue-and-groove on one side—and painted*!) Mary was Post Mistress for twenty-seven years, working out of the home. She also made 13 weather observations a day (recording visibility, temperature and precipitation.) Oh yes, she even milked the goats when Babe, normally home at night, was held up due to weather. Tanalian Bible Camp would come into being and the population of Port Alsworth would grow—from four tent frames to a population exceeding 200 people.

Babe flew the SR-JR to Egegik quite often, taking milk and produce to the Willis family. Before they left for Egegik, Babe flew the T-craft (Little Black Bird) to Nondalton—where one of the young Willis children prayed—asking the Lord to "please put it on Babe's heart to bring more bacon." (smile!)

Pilots and planes carry an amazing history, and we've appreciated the hard work and endurance of the pilots—whose incentives to go the extra mile accomplished so very much. We, Flo and Doris, have appreciated the *privilege* of watching the stately SR-JR plane in the air—and landing. We always *looked to the sky* to see who was flying overhead—and we still do!

In the spring of 1947, Mike VanDegrift had flown a silver and blue Taylor Craft N96012 from Austin, Minnesota to Alaska, selling the T-Craft to Babe for $1100. Many years later, Ralph Nabinger ended up with the black T-craft when Babe sold it to him—payment for work on their house in Hawaii. Ralph later sold it, possibly to Tommy O'Hara? It was eventually hauled back to Port Alsworth, and lost in the hanger fire—along with the wolf coats, the coyote coat, and the two sheep blankets. (Babe bought a new red T-Craft in MN in the 1970's.)

Babe had a great mechanic in Mike VanDegrift. According to historian John Branson, of Lake Clark National Park and Preserve, Mike VanDegrift was "universally known as a mechanical genius. He was equally at home working with metal or wood."

Bee, from the age of six, had observed Mike's mechanical skill—following him, asking questions, and helping when permitted. In time, younger brother, Johnny, followed along, learning from Bee and Mike, growing his interest in plane parts and engines.

On The Move

Mike VanDegrift was still at the farm when Flo and Doris came through the Lake Country in 1959 and 1960. Doris was dropped off at Port Alsworth by Arctic Mission's pilot, Dean Thimsen. Babe would see that she got to Pedro Bay. After the meal, Babe told Lonny to take Doris to Pedro Bay. (*I didn't know it was Lonny's solo flight on floats. However, I enjoyed the flight, and Lonny excelled!*) Mike left the area sometime around 1961, and Bee, though young, became ably prepared to continue skilled and knowledgeable maintenance on airplanes.

Flo and Doris moved to the village of Nondalton in 1965, after Harlan and Avanelle's move to Egegik. Arctic Missions was looking for someone to place in Nondalton; we offered, knowing a man and wife team would well-suit Pedro Bay. We had been in Alaska nearly five years—Flo stationed at Pedro Bay her first five years in Alaska—while Doris was stationed at South Naknek, Tanana, Kokhanok and Pedro Bay—consecutive years. Together, we'd move to Nondalton.

We were looking forward to furlough and seeing family. Still, it was hard to leave the village people, and it took a lot of preparation to ready the storage or pack for plane. Lonny stopped by our Nondalton house shortly before we left. We didn't realize it at the time, but it would be our last visit with Lonny this side of Heaven, for his Super Cub went down (ten minutes out of Iliamna) near Lower Talarik Creek (August, 1969), three souls aboard. What tragic loss—and how difficult for two little boys who would eventually hear of the plane accident that claimed their Daddy's life. Rumor, speculation, strong opinion—none could give a clear reason for the sudden loss. Ken and Vivian Hughes, of Arctic Missions, Inc. flew to Nondalton and Iliamna to conduct the memorial services. *Lonny would be sorely missed! In fact, he still is!*

More later, but for now, back to Leon and Sig!

Suits Skates
And Sourdoughs

Dick Proenneke, you had a great surprise
package sent to the boys from Wisconsin.
OshKosh B'Gosh, founded in 1895, manufactured
hickory striped denim bib overalls for the rail-
road—conductor hats as well. The little replica
suits made the three and five-year-old Alsworth
boys feel so special—as they truly were! Thanks,
Dick Proenneke, for being such a special friend to
two *very* special little boys!

We remember another package that came in the
mail for Leon and Sig. It was a gift that Grandma
Mary ordered—one of those early years around
Christmas time—two pair of leather, steel-bladed
ice-skates from the catalog! The family owned a
movie camera at the time, and the movie that came
forth from those ice-skates is still treasured.

We still laugh hard in remembrance! This was
the first time the boys had skates on their feet. Sig
was glad to hold someone's hand. Leon? That was a

different story. Leon insisted he already knew how to skate. Flo offered a broom he could hold onto, hoping it would offer some balance. Of course, he *didn't need it*. So, it was up-down, up-down, up-down continuously. That ice had to be hard, but we were glad he didn't have far to fall. Up on those little short legs—then down on his seat of learning, thrusting his skate-clad feet in the air! We laughed so hard our sides hurt; at the same time, we tried to hide our amusement, not wanting to intimidate Leon III, nor hurt his feelings! We were entertained so royally! I hope that short footage still exists. In time, Leon became steady on his feet. He enjoyed hockey, having played in High School and after. He must have been very good at it, too!

Dick, you always enjoyed your sourdough pancakes. The original starter probably came from Mary's sourdough pot. Grandpa Babe had an open-door policy when it came to the many pilots and passengers. Grandpa Babe and Mary were always great with hospitality. The planes would land on Grandpa's airstrip, needing to gas up before heading to Bristol Bay or the other direction through the pass. They were often forced to land and wait for weather to clear before they could go on. Babe and Mary didn't seem to mind (though there were times they could host 100 people a day!) Sourdough pancakes—along with Grandpa's thick-sliced bacon—made a wonderful breakfast for hungry people who were overnight guests. Grandpa Babe could fly two trips a day to Anchorage—dependent on weather conditions and daylight hours. (Today, with technology, Glen's planes can make four trips a day, flying 200 people a day—IFR not necessary.) Did I forget Grandma's warm home-made maple syrup? (Two cups sugar, one cup water. Heat and stir until the sugar dissolves. Add one teaspoon mapleine flavoring.)

THE FARM

W onder why it is called *The Farm*?? According to the children's growing up years, Grandpa Babe must have been as much farmer at heart as he was a pilot, for they had two horses (in 1952), goats, sheep, ducks, geese, chickens, turkey, guinea hen, bantam-rooster and hens, cats and dog. Sis remembers he had to fly to Levelock where the school-teacher, John Meggitt, was storing his order of grain, oats and mash for the animals. He would fly the Navion in *moonlight*, land on the frozen Kvichak river, load the big supply of animal food and take off, getting home before daylight sun could melt the ice, causing problems with take-off and landings.

Each visit made to Port Alsworth was memorable. We were privileged to help with cooking, baking, setting table, scrubbing floors, washing clothes—wherever a helping hand was needed. Mary prepared her own smoke-house salmon, but we were allowed to assist in the canning. Our time was much more than work, for the fellowship of the community and the privilege of helping Mary was good for us! We learned a lot from Mary—especially at fall-time when it came to preparing moose for the freezer. She taught us proper cuts of meat, and how best to wrap it to prevent freezer-burn. Sis remembers cutting and canning moose with Mary—usually in August. There's much we can say about moose—but let's save that for another Volume, ok??

One day, Babe and Mary found it necessary to make a trip to Anchorage and Portland, OR. Johnny was facing a serious health problem, which was eventually diagnosed. (Thank the Lord for Doctors—and especially when needed!) Flo and Doris were asked to run the farm until their return. Mary taught Flo to run the post-office and give the weather report—so important for pilots flying through Lake Clark Pass. Since there was no telephone, the report was made by radio, station KXC54 which was operated from Mary's post-office space in the Alsworth home. Flo learned to read the clouds and signs of daily weather. Doris' responsibility was to feed the chickens making sure they didn't escape. Babe had sacks full of *chicken-feed* (hard corn). It wasn't hard to feed the chickens, but the door must remain closed lest they get out. As for the goats, they were harder to feed.

There were burlap gunnysacks filled with rolled oats for the goats. The oats were scooped into a galvanized water pail, and though the goats were fenced, they seemed to know when their pail of food was headed their way. The lively, hungry goats all wanted to be first at the bucket! Feeding them one by one was impossible! How did Grandpa do it! I could just see myself knocked down and trampled. I lifted the pail, climbed over the fence, and ran as fast as two traumatized feet could run, the goats chasing after me. I dumped the oats, ran back to the fence—and bolted over. Though that little chore was somewhat difficult, the milking proved to be harder. I, Doris, knew I could milk the goats. I had grown up on a farm—remember? I had milked cows, and had even been kicked a few times. I knew how to hobble them, and I knew how to sit on a single, two or three-legged stool. The cows were milked from the side—and there was usually plenty to hold on to. Ones' head or shoulder could even be supported by leaning on the cow— unless she was mean and didn't like you! But it had been a long time since I had milked cows, and Babe's goats were milked from behind. They didn't have much to hold on to. After a cow was milked, you stripped any milk that was left—until she was milked dry. These goats were used to Babe's strong hands. When Babe and Mary's plane finally returned, I felt rescued—for my hands didn't feel capable of milking another goat!

> SCRIPTURE: *"And whatever you do, in word or deed, do all in the name of the Lord Jesus, giving thanks to God the Father through Him." Colossians 3:17*

Chicken And Eggs— Goats And Goat-Milk

Each year, Grandma and Grandpa would order some cute, fluffy baby chicks—up to 200 at a time—some for neighbors! They'd fixed a neat little box-pen right there in the kitchen—not far from the warm kitchen wood-stove. It was fun to watch them. Eventually, when old enough, they would be moved to the hen-house where a light-bulb was used for heat—until they were big enough to place among the flock. When the old layers *wore out*, Grandma served them up for Sunday best roast chicken! If too old and tough, they made great chicken soup! Regardless, the little chicks grew up to take their place—providing fresh eggs for the menu, whether sourdoughs or Grandma's special chocolate cake! Can you imagine how many fifty-pound sacks of flour and other staples it took to feed so many people? Thank God for Grandpa and his airplanes! Oh yes, the attached goat-barn provided winter heat and happy chickens—and chicken happiness was good nitrogen for rhubarb plants! Just ask Aunt Betty!

Goat's milk was another nutritious item on Grandma and Grandpa's table! Having come from a farm myself, I was use to cow's milk. The thought of drinking *goat's* milk wasn't such a great idea for me. My first trip through Lake Clark Pass required a stop at Port Alsworth. I was too polite to refuse the tall glass of goat milk set before me. I didn't want to gag—nor did I want to throw up! I held my breath and drank as much as I could—before catching my breath. I hadn't realized, chilled, well-cared-for goats milk—coming from well-fed, well-cared-for goats—was good for you—and could possibly taste good, too, especially when it was well-cared for and chilled. When I first met Margaret, she was such a vivacious little girl—striding toward the goat barn to show me how she milked the goats! I had her by the hand, and she seemed so solid-firm and strong!

Several years later, Leon and Sig were seated at our *own* breakfast table—eating our sourdough hotcakes—made from Grandma's given starter. We had poured—and set before them—tall glasses of cold goat milk. We found we could keep the goat milk cold by propping the filled milk-jar among the rocks in the small creek that ran alongside of our property. That, of course, was in summer. When the creek started to freeze up with winter coming on, the milk jar was set on the wind-break shelf. When the wind-break showed signs of freezing, we set the jar inside of the house, hoping to keep it drinkable! Anyway, Leon lifted his glass and took a good drink of cold goat's milk. What was left on his upper lip was a distinct "got-milk" mustache! I commented, *"Leon, you're just like a little goat."* His come-back truly sounded like one: *"Baaa!"*

Leon and Sig memorized Psalm 34:8, 9: *"Oh, taste and see that the Lord is good. Blessed is the man that trusts in Him!* Flo and Doris decided to memorize the whole Psalm—beneficial to this very day!

Garden And Greens

The goats and chickens contributed food for the Alsworth table. They also furnished fertilizer for the yearly planting of potatoes. Babe had a tractor and equipment for working the soil, and invited us to help at planting and harvest time.

The potato patch was large enough to warrant an invitation to other individuals and families as well. It was around this time we met Dick Proenneke! Dick arrived in the area around 1968, and was quick to give a hand. You have probably seen some of his beautiful camera work on National TV—showing the beautiful scene's around Twin Lakes. Perhaps you have read the book "One Man's Wilderness" or seen footage of his cabin and the wild animals. That is the Dick Proenneke who was quick to help Babe repair heavy equipment, grade the runway—or even plant and harvest potatoes. He was very much appreciated by Babe, for he didn't mind hard work. The potatoes were planted (by hand) a foot or so apart and two inches deep—and were hilled up as they grew. They were to stay in the ground until fall when the plant froze down to only an inch of green stem. *Many hands make the work lighter*, isn't that what we were told years ago???

This field of potatoes not only fed Babe and Mary's family, but the many pilots and passengers, neighbors and friends or strangers who graced their table. All were blessed of God through Babe and Mary, their family and farm! What a special team, caring for so many people!

I've tried to tell you about this amazing couple. We admired both Babe and Mary, but must admit, it is a bit complicated to explain Babe (smile). He was an individual thinker, and we'd be careful about our opinions lest in voicing them they would echo back from Babe's point of view (grin). One couldn't read his mind—just his grin! We learned to listen well and choose our words wisely. He was sharp, witty and wise—more often than not. One might say he was opinionated—especially when it came to FAA. Babe was well-studied on rules and regulations— but he didn't understand why they didn't agree with his thinking! Having flown his little black Taylor-craft for 25 years or so, it was well-prepared for hauling freight or people, landing on airstrip or sand-bar—in sunshine, rain or snow—whatever!

He knew his plane, and how and when to fly. He had not crashed it in his years of flying. The one thing we could safely express—often over a big bowl of popcorn—was the Scripture! We could always depend on God's Truth, for it was absolute. We have been so very privileged to have Babe and Mary—and their family—in our lives! Now, back to Mary, our true sister in the Lord!

Babe with his T-craft at Nondalton

Mary's Greenhouse gave an early spring-start for cabbage, cauliflower, beets, swiss-chard, broccoli, celery and lettuce. Carrot, parsnip, onion, pre-sprouted peas and beans were usually planted directly into the garden soil. Mary ordered seed from State-side in time for spring planting. She used commercial fertilizer at times, and the watering barrel was always kept full of water and warmed by the sun, ready for the thirsty plants. We enjoyed transplanting from greenhouse to garden. We enjoyed weeding and hoeing the garden—and hilling the potato plants. But we especially enjoyed helping Mary in the kitchen. We, along with other hungry workers, enjoyed the bounty set before us! When it was time to return home, we were given a generous supply of produce to take along. For the three school-years Leon and Sig were with us, their Grandpa and Grandma made sure we had garden produce, meat and milk on our Nondalton table.

SCRIPTURE:

> *"And my God shall supply all your need, according to His riches in Glory by Christ Jesus" Philippians 4:1*

"I am the DOOR." "I am the Good Shepherd. The Good Shepherd giveth His life for the sheep." "I know My sheep and am known by My own" John 10:7-30.

"He who knew no sin became sin for us that we may become the righteous-ness of God in Him." "For God so loved the world that He gave His only begotton Son, that WHOSOEVER believeth in Him should not perish, but have everlasting life. For God sent not His Son into the world to condemn the world, but that the world, through Him, might be saved." John 3:16, 17

Bread, Butter, Cranberries And Dry-Fish

Mary made wonderful sourdoughs, but she also made big batches of wonderful home-made bread, serving it with a pass-around plate of real butter! The butter came in one-pound blocks, salt-brined in a keg. The canneries at Bristol Bay used the same in their cook houses. The brined butter didn't turn rancid easily and was probably shipped up from Seattle by boat. (One could also purchase cases of canned butter or canned milk.) We still use Mary's white and/or brown bread recipe, as does Mary's daughter, and most probably her grand-daughters! If it was a good year for berries, the wild low-bush cranberry (lingonberry) was a favorite jam or sauce at nearly every meal. On plentiful years, Mary canned two-gallon jars of cranberry sauce: 1 cup water, 9 cups berries—bring to a boil, boil 1 minute, then jar and seal. Tip hot jar upside down for about five minutes, then upright. The canning-lid should seal. It is very rewarding to hear the lids pop and seal! It is even more rewarding to place the sealed jars on the storage shelves for winter! Add sugar when you open the jar: 1 cup sugar to 1 cup sauced berries. She also made cranberry jam adding pectin and sugar before jarring. It took many hours to pick, clean and can those tiny berries, but berry-picking should be fun! Take lunch along and share it with friends—a true picnic! So much can be said for Alaska's berries and the outdoors!

Bread has been an all-occasion staple for any meal. It is known as the staff of life. You can always put bread and jam on the table—along with a cup of tea. Add some canned salmon or smoked-salmon-strips, and you have a gourmet meal! Mary, her daughter, Margaret (Sis,) and her daughters-in-law—Betty, Esther and Patty—put up great dry-fish which could be hung in the cache, stored in the freezer or canned and shelved in the pantry. *Leon, I well-remember bear-claw and teeth-marks on your Aunt Betty's smoke house—way above our reach!* According to Betty, Bee along with Tony B. and Glen V. were able, with the help of a barking dog, to detect and shoot the nine-foot-tall brown-bear—securing safety.

Our Daily Bread (ourdailybread.org) is a devotional we've ordered and used for around 60 years. PO Box 2222, Grand Rapids, MI 49501-2222. After Grandma Mary's conversion, Grandpa brought the daily reading to their family table!

VILLAGE VISITORS
AND INTERVENTION

I t was a special time of year when Ken and Vivian
Hughes came to our village for Gospel Meetings.
We loved having them. Villagers across Alaska
enjoyed their ministry—including their *Gypsy Boy
Song* and Ken's special slight-of-hand antics with a
quarter or ping-pong ball. Vivian would tell a flash-
card story about the upside-down-frown. Ken and
Vivian would share the song about *Captain Johnson*,
then Ken would share a message from the Bible.

One particular evening—the night of their
arrival—we invited them to the village meeting
which was already under way—about a ten-minute
walk away from our home. They opted not to go, so
we—Flo, Doris, Leon and Sig—stayed home with
them, enjoying the good visit we knew we would
have. Hopefully they could rest up from their flight.
We were seated in our kitchen area. Suddenly, the
power-plant—otherwise known as a light-plant—
began to surge. The lights were dimming and the

power fluctuating. Surely, we hadn't failed to add diesel oil to the tank!? We rounded the corner of the house to hear our 2½ KW Lister-Diesel threatening to quit. Smoke was billowing from the left side of the light-plant shed. Ken rushed in to turn it off—unable to find the shut-off lever. Doris bounded in, turned it off, and bounded out. While Ken was busy with the problem, Flo ran for the water buckets. We rounded up a flashlight for Leon and Sig—with instructions to find neighbors Pete and Ruth or any other fast emergency help.

The boys took off bare-footed, as fast as their little, short legs could carry them! They returned with Johnny and Arsenie, who so skillfully wielded an axe—chopping into the five-or-six-inch-thick sawdust-filled wall. In the earlier days, sawdust was not only used for insulation in the walls of buildings, but also for storing block-ice, or mixing with fuel for fire-starter (being careful what kind of fuel to use and knowing how to use it, as you don't want it to blow up!!) The heavy 4-inch exhaust pipe attached to our 2 ½ KW light-plant had a hole worn in it from years of vibration. Hot exhaust had caused the sawdust to smolder—how long, we didn't know, but it finally burst into flame! The problem had affected the wiring, too, causing electricity failure, and plant shut down. Thankfully, we had some stored water on hand. How good it was that *Ken and Vivian* had come—*Johnny* and *Arsenie*, having skipped the village meeting were nearby—and *Leon and Sig* knew how to run fast!

Thank you, Lord, for your mercy, care, and intervention—diverting further disaster; sparing our light-plant, our home—and other village homes should the fire have spread. Leon and Sig, what a blessing you have been to all of us!!

Leon and Krissi

Leon And Krissi—Today!

Leon III met and married Krissi Painter—a beautiful lady with a beautiful singing voice. God blessed them with a son, Leon IV (Trapper), and a grand-son, Leon V, and grand-daughter, Yarrow! Also, two daughters, Tanalian and Tazimina (known as Kaylee). Leon III has worked a number of years as a pilot for the National Park Service, stationed at Lake Clark/Port Alsworth, having logged approximately 14,000 hours of flight time. He is now retired, and we are waiting the day he and Krissy can come visit *the mission girls*!

Remembrance

Leon III remembers his mother, Martha Bedell Alsworth, leading him to the Lord—before he moved to Grandpa and Grandma's house. She was present at his High-School Graduation. She remarried, sometime after, and lived in Alaska a few more years—giving Leon two special brothers, Josh and Jamie. Sadly, Martha became a *missing person*—found in 1996. Martha had given us a special piece of Lake Clark drift-wood on which she had painted a verse: *"As for God His Way is Perfect" (*Psalm *18:30).* There were also forget-me-nots of yellow, red, white and blue! We gave the plaque over to Leon several years ago, and trust the verse will be a positive remembrance, not only of his mother, but of the Lord's sure Hand upon his life. *"The Word of the Lord is proven; He is a shield to all who trust in Him."*

Sig Rodney Alsworth was working as a fishing guide when he was unexpectedly called Home to God's House—September 17, 1982.

SOMEDAY IN GOD'S GREAT HEAVEN

In memory of Sig Rodney Alsworth
1965–1982

Our Lord knows every sorrow
He sees and feels the pain
He gives us new tomorrows
And softly falling rain.

Someday in God's great Heaven
We'll know the reasons why
All tears will be forgotten
There'll be no need to cry.
Our Savior is the Sunshine
The Door that opens wide
And Sig will be there Smiling
So blessed to be Inside!

Dh

See you!

Mary Agnes Griechen Alsworth:
August 9, 1924 - September 26, 1996

Leon Reid Alsworth:
April 13, 1909 - October 6, 2004

CPSIA information can be obtained
at www.ICGtesting.com
Printed in the USA
FSHW022133150719

9 781545 659229